PURE MILK

NURTURING NEW LIFE IN JESUS

BRIAN JOHNSTON

Pure Milk: Nurturing New Life in Jesus

Unless otherwise indicated, all Scripture quotations are from the HOLY BIBLE, the New King James Version® (NKJV®). Copyright © 1982 Thomas Nelson, Inc. Used by permission. All rights reserved. Scriptures marked NIV are from New International Version®, NIV® Copyright © 1973, 1978, 1984, 2011 by Biblica, Inc.™ Used by permission. All rights reserved worldwide. Scriptures marked NASB are from the New American Standard Bible®, Copyright © 1960, 1962, 1963, 1968, 1971, 1972, 1973, 1975, 1977, 1995 by The Lockman Foundation Used by permission. (www.Lockman.org)

Published by Hayes Press (**www.hayespress.org**)

Book and Cover design by Hayden Press. For information contact : haydenpress2011@gmail.com

If you enjoy reading this book, please consider taking a moment to leave a positive review on Amazon.

ISBN: 9781871126211

First Edition : January 2016

10 9 8 7 6 5 4 3 2 1

CONTENTS

1: THE BEGINNING OF A RELATIONSHIP WITH JESUS

The Apostle Paul didn't only preach and lead people to Christ, he also invested himself in their lives. To see that, you only need to read 1 Thessalonians 2:7-11 where he tells us he was as gentle and fondly affectionate as a nursing mother in all his care for new converts. He really poured himself into the process of seeing them grow and develop spiritually. The words that follow are Paul's expressing of his ambition for those who had come to faith at Colossae: "We proclaim [Christ], admonishing every man and teaching every man with all wisdom, so that we may present every man complete in Christ" (Colossians 1:28).

The stated aim of that verse is for each new Christian to become mature. It's something 'caught' as well as 'taught' from

Scripture as we absorb the examples in the narrative of the Bible story-line. Where would Paul have been without Ananias - or Barnabas for that matter (see Acts 9:1-19; Acts 11:19-26); and where would Timothy, Priscilla and Aquila have been without Paul (see Acts 16:1-3; Acts 18:1-3)? This mentoring process is more than chats over a cup of coffee – although it will likely include that – and it's also more than the delivery of instruction: it's an intentional process of being nurtured in the new life which we have in Jesus, and it happens when we benefit from one-on-one interactions with a more mature Christian disciple who spends time in helping us to become nourished in the Christian faith (see 1 Timothy 4:6; John 21:15-17). Obviously, it's two-way, in that the novice Christian asks advice from the more experienced mentor – perhaps about such things as how to pray and how to read the Bible in a meaningful way.

An important aspect of mentoring is finding someone who can be a positive role model for us. I never had any formal mentoring, sadly, but I definitely did single out one or two persons at different times in my formative spiritual experience. I would make every effort to be present when they were scheduled to teach God's Word, and – perhaps unconsciously at times – I allowed myself to be influenced by their values, and even tried in some way to emulate how they lived for the Lord.

The Bible doesn't use the word 'mentor' but it has a word translated either as 'ensamples' or 'examples' (it's the same meaning; e.g. 1 Thessalonians 1:7; 2 Thessalonians 3:9; Philippians 3:17; 1 Timothy 4:12, Titus 2:7, 'tupos', 'become a pattern'). It's used to describe those who were positive role models: whose lives were worth copying – as you would copy from a pattern. So, these were men or women who were 'pattern disciples,' setting a good standard in behaviour and in practice for all aspects of the Christian life. Paul spoke of "offer[ing] ourselves as a model for you, so that you would follow our example" (2 Thessalonians 3:9).

Now how might someone who wanted to help a new Christian set about doing that? Well, surely it would be good to begin at the beginning, reminding the person who's recently received Christ of exactly what it is that's happened to him or her. And what was that? In the words of John 3:3 – and they are Jesus' own words – he or she has been 'born again.' Our friend has been born as a Christian – as that's the only way to become one.

The natural birth of a child is usually a cause of joy to its parents and to all their friends. It's the beginning of another life. Another person is born, with all the possibilities that life holds. The new birth is a greater occasion than any natural birth, because it's the beginning of eternal life – life without end. When a child is born, its name is recorded in a book on earth, but when we are born again our names are recorded in heaven (Luke 10:20). When a person receives Christ by faith as his or her personal saviour (John 1:12), the new birth takes place by the Spirit of God (John 3:5-6) in the person who believes what the Word of God has to say about them and about Christ (1 Peter 1:23).

Our new life has come about by our being identified in faith with Jesus' death. We did this when we realized he died under our judgment. The death sentence he served on the cross was ours before a holy God. In his death we have our new birth. The Bible encourages us to understand Jesus as having been raised from the dead, and we with him. In fact, it says:

"Therefore if you have been raised up with Christ, keep seeking the things above, where Christ is, seated at the right hand of God. Set your mind on the things above, not on the things that are on earth. For you have died and your life is hidden with Christ in God. When Christ, who is our life, is revealed, then you also will be revealed with Him in glory. Therefore, consider the members of your earthly body as dead to immorality, impurity, passion, evil desire, and greed, which amounts to idolatry. For it is because of these things that the wrath of God will come upon the sons of disobedience, and in them you also once walked, when you were living in them. But now you also, put them all aside: anger, wrath, malice, slander, and abusive speech from your mouth.

Do not lie to one another, since you laid aside the old self with its evil practices, and have put on the new self who is being renewed to a true knowledge according to the image of the One who created him. So, as those who have been chosen of God, holy and beloved, put on a heart of compassion, kindness, humility, gentleness and patience; bearing with one another, and forgiving each other, whoever has a complaint against anyone; just as the Lord forgave you, so also should you. Beyond all these things put on love, which is the perfect bond of unity" (Colossians 3:1-14).

In other words, since we have new life in Jesus, through his death on the cross, we should now have newer and higher thoughts and ambitions, consistent with the idea of Jesus now being enthroned in heaven. In turn, this should lead to new desires and new behaviours in the way we live our lives, meaning we should decisively put an end to past practices that are unworthy of our new identity in Christ.

When Paul wrote his Bible letter to the Philippians, he expressed his strong desire for them in the first chapter, that they should be able to discern what's best in life (Philippians 1:10) and decide to go after that with everything they had. In the rest of the letter, Paul devotes space to helping them identify exactly what is best in life. He shares his own experience, as their mentor:

"… I count all things to be loss in view of the surpassing value of knowing Christ Jesus my Lord, for whom I have suffered the loss of all things, and count them but rubbish so that I may gain Christ, … that I may know Him and the power of His resurrection and the fellowship of His sufferings, being conformed to His death; … I press on so that I may lay hold of that for which also I was laid hold of by Christ Jesus. Brethren, I do not regard myself as having laid hold of it yet; but one thing I do: forgetting what lies behind and reaching forward to what lies ahead, I press on toward the goal for the prize of the upward call of God in Christ Jesus. Brethren, join in following my example, and observe those who walk according to the pattern you have in us … For our citizenship is in heaven, from which also we eagerly wait for a Savior, the Lord Jesus Christ." (Philippians 3:8-14,17,20)

The New Testament word for "to serve as a deacon" can mean to wait upon or to serve tables. I began my latest time in the Philippines by sitting to down to breakfast upon my early morning arrival. A waiter, previously known to me, approached the table I was sitting at, and rather than asking 'How are your eggs and rice?' he asked: 'How's your relationship with God?' The directness and openness of the culture there is refreshing. It's a good question with which to begin each day. Christianity is first and foremost a relationship with Jesus Christ. We take the pulse of our own experience by checking if the deepest longing of our hearts is the same as the Apostle Paul's, which was 'That I may know him' (Philippians 3:10).

In a similar way, the Old Testament writer spoke of how nothing in his life compared to the Lord; of how there was nothing on earth he desired more than the Lord. Paul spoke of 'the surpassing value of knowing Christ' (Philippians 3:8). In that context, he spoke about 'forgetting the things that are behind' (Philippians 3:13). How often we hear this quoted as a mere encouragement to move on from some negative experience, when in reality it's describing all the highlights of Saul of Tarsus' pre-conversion life!

The things now lying behind Paul were honourable things in themselves, and much prized by the world, but compared with the all-consuming experience of knowing Christ, they were like (so Paul effectively said) what we might scrape from our shoe when we've trodden on something undesirable on the street. That's the graphic imbalance between all this world desires, and wars to own, compared with the surpassing value of knowing Christ. We remind ourselves of how the apostles spoke of David seeing the Lord always in his presence (Acts 2:25). Only such a fine-toned devotional life will succeed in keeping us from temptation.

Paul was writing these words at that time from his prison in the capital city of the Roman Empire. And he was writing to what was a distant colonial city, the city of Philippi. It was populated by many retired soldiers who were fiercely loyal to the Emperor of Rome. So, the city of Philippi was a colony or outpost of Rome and its Empire. Its citizens lived there by the values and customs of faraway Rome. Paul uses that fact as an illustration of the reality that we Christians are an outpost of heaven here on this earth. We should live by the values and laws of heaven, and not by the fashion and opinions of the changing world around us which has largely turned its back on God.

Well, that sets our compass in the direction we're headed. Our next step in exploring the Christian life will be to present the biblical case for total assurance of our salvation.

2: HOW CAN I BE SURE IT'S REALLY TRUE?

To read the Apostle John's letters is to enter another world, a world whose characteristic marks are assurance, confidence and certainty. It's here we find a resounding theme of Christian certainty. And, according to John, Christian certainty is a double certainty. First, the certainty that Christianity itself is true. This is about objective facts: things rooted in history. A baby was born in the obscure Middle Eastern town of Bethlehem. He learned the trade of carpentry. One day he shut the doors of the carpentry shop and became an itinerant preacher despite having no recognized formal schooling, as such. His life was reportedly full of wonders, his teaching incomparable, and he claimed to be equal with God, but still he gained no mass acceptance, and was executed in a criminal's death by those jealous of him.

On the third day thereafter, his few followers claimed they saw him risen from the dead. The rest, as they say, is history – no other life has impacted the planet in the same way, testimony to the truth - as John claims - that this was God come in humanity.

And the Apostle John opens his first letter by referencing the reality of those historical facts underpinning the Christian faith: "That which was from the beginning, which we have heard, which we have seen with our eyes, which we have looked upon, and our hands have handled, concerning the Word of life ... the life was manifested, and we have seen, and bear witness, and declare to you that eternal life which was with the Father and was manifested to us ... that which we have seen and heard we declare to you, that you also may have fellowship with us; and truly our fellowship is with the Father and with His Son Jesus Christ. And these things we write to you that your joy may be full" (1 John 1:1-4 NKJV).

According to John, genuine faith must draw authentically on 'that which is from the beginning' - those defining historic events which reset the clocks some 2,000 years ago. He goes on to write about the birth, baptism and death of Jesus when he writes that: "... Jesus Christ has come in the flesh ... He ... came by water and blood ... [in a reference to his baptism and death] ... And we know that the Son of God has come and has given us an understanding, that we may know Him who is true; and we are in Him who is true, in His Son Jesus Christ. This is the true God and eternal life" (1 John 4:2; 5:5,6,20 NKJV).

Altogether, in John's writing, there are three assurances given for the certainty of Christian truth. First, there's what we've just been mentioning – the actual historical events of the life of Jesus Christ. Then there's the witness of the apostles. John has already, as we have seen, appealed to the direct experience of the apostles in their encounter with Jesus Christ by talking of 'the life was manifested, and we have seen, and bear witness'. And thirdly,

John mentions 'the anointing from the Holy One' which enables Christian believers to know the truth, especially the truth about Jesus Christ (1 John 2:20-27). In this way, John is referring to the gift of the Holy Spirit which every person receives at conversion when they become a believer on Christ. He's the Spirit of truth and guides us into all the truth, as Jesus himself promised, and recorded by John in his Gospel (in John 16:13).

Christianity is therefore firmly anchored to historical realities, and is confirmed not only by the inner testimony of the Holy Spirit within Christians, but also by the witness of the apostles who'd actually been with him and so could vouch for the objective historical reality of events like the resurrection. Those are the three great assurances John gives for the truth of Christianity: the assurance of history, of the apostles, and of the Holy Spirit.

So much then for the certainty of the truth of Christianity – although we might add that lawyers and historians have famously declared Jesus' resurrection to be the best supported fact in all history. But moving on now, to the other certainty that the apostle John writes about in his letters, especially this first letter … it concerns the Christian's assurance of personally belonging to God's family and being the possessor of eternal life. So there's a beautiful balance in the double certainty presented by John in his letters, covering on the one hand, the objective truth of the historical foundations of the Christian faith; while also affirming the subjective experience of the Christian believer's personal convictions.

And John also gives three assurances for the second certainty he presents: which is the certainty of knowing, through faith, that we've been born into God's spiritual family and, as a result, possess eternal life. John's repeated message is that those who 'believe' may 'know'. In chapter 2 verse 3, he speaks of 'knowing Him (Jesus)' and then goes on to speak of 'knowing that we are in Him' (v.5); and later of 'knowing we are of God and of the truth (1 John 5:19; 4:6; 3:19). Finally, in his last chapter, he speaks about 'knowing that we have eternal life' (1 John 5:13). You see what I mean about his theme being 'knowing with certainty'?

But how is it possible to have this absolute knowledge? Many people speak of hoping they'll be acceptable to God and one day enter into life in God's presence. John, however, writes about knowledge that's certain. He gives, as we've said, three ways by which we can be sure that we're already eternally secure: and these are by believing, by obeying and by loving.

The first way is about maintaining our deep conviction in the truth about Jesus, the Son of God. Again and again in chapter five alone, he stresses that it's those who 'believe in the Son of God' (vv.5,10,13) who know they have eternal life. He emphasizes that assurance comes by remaining in what they've heard from the beginning (1 John 2:24). Sadly, some believers, by losing faith, lose the assurance of their salvation - even though they can't lose salvation itself.

The second assurance is by means of keeping the Lord's commands and doing the things that are right (1 John 3:9,10). Among the things John writes aimed at helping us really know that we have eternal life (1 John 5:13) is this matter of keeping the Lord's commandments: "…everyone who loves Him who begot also loves him who is begotten of Him. By this we know that we love the children of God, when we love God and keep His commandments." (1 John 5:1-2 NKJV)

Earlier, as though to reinforce that, he's already said: "Whoever has been born of God does not sin, for His seed remains in him; and he cannot sin, because he has been born of God. In this the children of God and the children of the devil are manifest: Whoever does not practice righteousness is not of God." (1 John 3:9-10 NKJV).

Now, it's not that this means we should be sinless, for John has already told us that 'if we say that we have no sin, we deceive ourselves'. What it means is that at the time of our conversion, a new nature was born within us. This new nature cannot sin, but we do still have the old nature which won't finally be removed until we're changed at the coming of Christ. However, consistent with the new nature, the practice of righteousness ought to characterize those who are God's children, and be typical of them. When that's the case, it all serves as further assurance to our own hearts that a work of God's grace has been done there.

The third way of assurance of someone having been born into God's family and possessing eternal life is by loving one another (1 John 4:7,8). Remember, John has said at the beginning of chapter five, we've mentioned it already, but we'll quote it again: "Whoever believes that Jesus is the Christ is born of God, and everyone who loves Him who begot also loves him who is begotten of Him (1 John 5:1 NKJV). To see how strongly this matter of loving one another comes over as an assurance of our new birth and possession of eternal life, we only have to read some more verses from the previous chapter:

"Beloved, let us love one another, for love is of God; and everyone who loves is born of God and knows God. He who does not love does not know God, for God is love." (1 John 4:7-8)

"If someone says, "I love God," and hates his brother, he is a liar; for he who does not love his brother whom he has seen, how can he love God whom he has not seen? And this commandment we have from Him: that he who loves God must love his brother also." (1 John 4:20-21 NKJV)

So now, let's sum up all that we've been saying. The Apostle John, in his first Bible letter, presents us with two certainties: the first being the objective historical truth of Christianity and the other being the subjective confidence that the Christian believer has eternal life. Each of these two certainties is supported by three assurances. The first certainty is assured by well-evidenced historical events; by the remarkable witness of the apostles; and by the gift of the Holy Spirit which every believer on the Lord Jesus Christ receives at conversion (please read carefully Romans 8:9,16). The second certainty – which is our confidence of actually having full forgiveness and lasting life from God – is also triply assured when we retain our convictions about the person of the Lord Jesus; and keep his commandments; and love each other.

How wonderful to have a strong, a threefold assurance of the certainty of having a place in God's family and of being the possessor of eternal life – something which no power in the universe can alter (see Romans 8:35-39 – please do read the 5 'guarantees' of vv.31-39 – namely that God is for us; sacrificing his own son to bless us, God himself being the one who justifies us, with the risen Jesus interceding for us, such that we have endless victory through God's love in Jesus).

Just so there's no misunderstanding, let me again say that John's theme is not how to obtain salvation, but the assurance of salvation. And also, even if we lose our assurance, we cannot lose our salvation itself (see John 10:28,29). In our early days as a Christian – and possibly many times later on – our enemy, the Devil, will try to deploy his original, devastating tactic of sowing doubt. Remember how he said to Eve in the Garden 'has God said …?' (Genesis 3:1). We can best prepare for that attack by entering John's world of certainty and assurance.

3: DISCOVERING THE BIBLE AS GOD'S MANUAL FOR LIFE

One of the first things we need to do when new to the experience of the Christian Faith is to ensure that we make time to nurture our relationship with the Lord through regular exposure to the nourishment of God's Word. To that end, it's quite important to discover how to read the Bible for all it's worth - and not only to read it - but to memorize verses and internalize their teaching – and, above all, to be delighted by it. We should also take steps to become convinced of the Bible's reliability and of its power to speak into our lives.

The Apostle Paul urged his protégé, Timothy, to pay attention to Bible-reading – and if that was in public, then how much more in private also (1 Timothy 4:13). The kings of Israel were commanded by God to read God's Word daily (Deuteronomy

17:18,19). The Lord himself, in his humanity, by his frequent quotation of the Old Testament, displayed clear evidence of memorisation that surely came from a reading habit. All of which means we should follow their example.

One Christian, speaking of the great value of the Bible for our daily living, said 'I learned years ago, to go to one place for the deepest lessons of life ... that one place is the Bible' (R. A. Torrey, former President of Moody Bible Institute). Life's best advice is found in the Bible: "How blessed is the man who does not walk in the counsel of the wicked, nor stand in the path of sinners, nor sit in the seat of scoffers! But his delight is in the law of the LORD, and in His law he meditates day and night. He will be like a tree firmly planted by streams of water, which yields its fruit in its season and its leaf does not wither; and in whatever he does, he prospers" (Psalm 1:1-3).

As new Christians, we'll want to learn how to navigate the storms of life; how to be productive for God; and how to discover the secret of spiritual health and vitality; not to mention getting to know the laws of spiritual success! Well, the first psalm points out the enormous benefit to be gained from reading God's Word, the Bible. For at the root of all these mentioned, desirable things in our spiritual bucket list is a daily Bible-reading habit. Using the imagery of a riverside tree, Psalm 1 assures us that love for the Word of God will result in us being 'firmly planted', yielding 'fruit', without withering, but always prospering. In other words, it's saying that a passion for Bible-reading will tend to promote in our lives a sense of stability, that is, being settled in our convictions; as well as being productive in our service; while experiencing vitality and prosperity – those latter qualities, of course, being primarily in the spiritual sense.

Personally, I well remember discovering the reality of that in my student life. I cherish with a deep fondness the recollection of evenings in my battered old car overlooking a reservoir at sunset, listening to Christian music on a rather scratchy stereo cassette player, while at the same time developing a passion for God through his Word as he was opening the Scriptures to me and opening my eyes, mind and heart to them. Those sunset 'tutorials' were the most impressive and influential I ever had during my time at university. The delight for God and his Word which he sparked in me then would lead to the later fulfilment of my heart desires in service, proving to me the thrilling reality of the promise in that later psalm: "Delight yourself in the LORD; and He will give you the desires of your heart" (Psalm 37:4).

We read to enjoy him. Delighting in God's Law (Psalm 1), or Bible, is closely connected with delighting in the Lord himself (Psalm 37). The two are inseparable. I would say that the most fulfilling experience in this life is proving that verse 4 of Psalm 37 is absolutely true: delighting in the Lord will bring about the fulfilment of our desires (because they'll have become transformed to be what God himself wants).

Just as we look through, not at, a microscope; so we read the Bible that we might get to know God better – the God of the Word is himself like the Word of God: ... Perfect, restoring the soul; sure, making wise the simple; right, rejoicing the heart; pure, enlightening the eyes; clean, enduring forever; true, righteous altogether (Psalm 19). It's such a thrill to get to know someone like that!

As we said, it'll help us if we can be sure that the Bible we have is true to the original form in which it was first communicated. It's well-known, and widely reported – so easy to check out – that from among all ancient literature nothing comes even remotely close to the Bible in passing the standard literary tests for a book being true to its original form. What's more, by making painstaking comparisons between thousands of early language fragments, experts, working like detectives, are able to make a strong case for knowing pretty well exactly what the original text of the Bible said – and based on that knowledge, we can be confident that our English language Bibles are reliable.

The Bible is such a special book from God. He's its ultimate author, and it's his revelation to us, affirmed by lots of its predictions having been fulfilled with exact precision. So, it's no doubt very special, but in the main we're meant to read it like any other book, taking its words to have their normal meanings. And it's not written much like a textbook: for much of the time God instructs us through narrating the life experiences of others. We begin to gain a clear sense of what God approves in their lives which we can then begin to apply in our own life. There's no situation in life for which we can't find guidance - at least in principle – from this vast store of human encounters with God. As we read its pages regularly, we'll find our attention is often drawn to certain statements it makes and we begin to sense their particular relevance to decisions we have pending, as well as to other of life's experiences. So, the greatest wonder of the Bible is that God speaks to us through its pages.

Two of the earliest followers of Jesus said in Luke 24:32: "Were not our hearts burning within us while He was speaking to us on the road, while He was explaining the Scriptures to us?" We, too, can have the same experience whenever we sit down with a mature Christian friend or with a reputable study book, and after asking the Lord's help in prayer, we begin to enjoy a time of Bible study. Long ago, using the parts of the Bible available to him then, the psalmist said: 'I ... see wonderful things ... from Your law' (Psalm 119:18).

That reminds me of how, after 15 years of financing excavations in the Valley of the Kings with scarcely anything to show for his expenditure, Lord Carnarvon began to wonder if it would all prove fruitless. But then came an excited telegram from Howard Carter telling him to come to Luxor immediately. On 26 November 1922, Carter and Lord Carnarvon stood in front of the sealed door of Tutankhamun's tomb. Carter made a small hole in the door and then inserted a candle. Answering Carnarvon's anxious question, "Can you see anything?" Carter famously replied, "Yes, wonderful things." And there are wonderful things to be discovered in the pages of our Bible. Things which will warm our hearts, feed our souls, and draw us into close fellowship with the Lord. These blessings will be ours if we approach our reading prayerfully, asking for the eyes of our heart to be opened in the Holy Spirit's working.

But life can get so busy, and we'll need to each make a conscious, deliberate lifestyle choice - just as Mary of Bethany did, as we read of her in Luke's Gospel chapter 10 and verse 39: Mary ... was seated at the Lord's feet, listening to His word ... And the Lord affirmed her action, by saying: 'Mary has chosen the good part' (Luke 10:39-42).

May we never forget just how valuable the Bible – and our daily reading of it – is. Dr Lehman Strauss talked about having 'The Word of God' stamped on the spine of his rebound Bible –

as an ever-present visible reminder that this was not just a book, but in reality 'The Word of God.' As such, it should have a unique place in all our lives. Thomas Aquinas is reputed to have used the Latin phrase "hominem unius libri timeo" (meaning "I fear the man of a single book"). But Aquinas' phrase was consciously turned on its head by John Wesley who said:

"He came from heaven; He hath written it down in a book. O give me that Book! At any price, give me the Book of God. I have it; here is knowledge enough for me. Let me be homo unius libri!" (or the man of one Book). John Wesley was certainly captivated by the Bible, so much so that one historian wrote of him: '... from the unlikely soil of a grossly immoral, drink-sodden nation of brutalized gamblers on the verge of collapse into absolute infidelity, [there] sprang under God and through Wesley the great awakening, the evangelical revival of the 18th century, which doubtless spared England a revolution such as befell the French' – such was the impact, under God, of only one man captivated by the Bible.

May we also be captivated by its pages! This is the formula for spiritual growth in the adventure of a Christian life recently begun … like newborn babies, long for the pure milk of the word, so that by it you may grow in respect to salvation (1 Peter 2:2). Read a little each day, read systematically, and occasionally study Bible characters and topics. Vary your diet with all parts of the Bible. Read, and grow in the grace and knowledge of the Lord you follow. And as we read, the promise is you and I will become more like him: "But we all, with unveiled face, beholding as in a mirror the glory of the Lord, are being transformed into the same image from glory to glory, just as from the Lord, the Spirit" (2 Corinthians 3:18).

4: LEARNING TO TALK WITH GOD

As well as the 'scripture experience' which we thought about in the previous chapter, we also need the 'sanctuary experience' - in other words, new and not-so-new Christians need to experience God's presence through prayer. In praying, it's helpful to learn from a child's basic words: 'sorry, thanks, please.' For example, in the psalms of the Bible - which are prayers after all - the four key responses that come up again and again are: 'Wow', 'Sorry', 'Thanks' and 'Help'.

Praying like that is the way God's chosen to bring his blessings to his children. It also emphasizes the personal relationship we have with God. More than that, in the act of praying we acknowledge that God is sovereign. That means we're to pray according to his will, and in line with his values. We're to pray with a clear conscience and a clean heart in conformity with God's character, and consistently with his revealed purposes. These are among the conditions for answered prayer and living in the joy of it. In that way, we claim in prayer those things which are his promises to us. But how do we go about it?

Where can we get to know God's will and what his values are? The Bible, of course. So, the more we can relate our prayer requests to what the Scriptures reveal, the better. We learn to turn biblical sentences into one-line prayers. Above all, we must always rely on the Holy Spirit's guidance: not only praying in the Word, but praying in the Spirit.

Many Christians use the expression 'having their Quiet Time' to mean the time they set aside each day for stilling their souls in the presence of God. When we prepare to enjoy fellowship with our Maker, it's good to shut ourselves off from a hundred and one everyday things that clutter our lives and minds. There's no better advice than the Lord's (Matthew 6:6) when he counselled us to have a particular place to retire to where we can be free from interruptions, where we can disentangle ourselves; from our daily duties; and from the worries and pressures that come with life. Two things which belong together are praying and watching (which includes ring-fencing our time commitment and looking out for answers).

I don't know whether your habit is to pray out loud or whether you pray silently during your personal prayers at home. The Bible records the Lord's instruction as being: 'When you pray 'say': Our Father in heaven etc.' It's often helpful to pray audibly even in private. To 'say' the prayer rather than to just 'think' it. I certainly find it's an aid to concentration when we actually put it into spoken words – it helps to guard against wandering thoughts or skating too glibly over a range of different issues without any real depth of thought. This habit is even a help when it comes to breaking the sound barrier of audible prayer with others.

It was the Lord Jesus himself who taught us in Matthew chapter 6: "When you pray, go into your room, and when you have shut your door, pray to your Father who is in the secret place; and your Father who sees in secret will reward you openly" (v.6 NKJV). But that doesn't always mean that praying comes naturally, as easy as breathing. The Bible itself recognizes there will be times when we don't know how to pray as we ought. And, if you're like me, from time to time you'll be jolted into realising just how shallow your prayer life has become. There may well be times too when we feel spiritually dry and not at all in the right frame of mind for praying. Of course, these are the times when we need prayer all the more. If we persevere with the discipline of prayer even when it feels more like a duty than genuine devotion, and speak to God about how we feel, we'll soon find the exercise once more becomes a delight.

The Lord's first followers said: 'Lord, teach us to pray.' In response the Lord gave them an example of praying with six major points: 'Our Father who is in heaven, Hallowed be Your name. Your kingdom come. Your will be done, on earth as it is in heaven. Give us this day our daily bread. And forgive us our debts, as we also have forgiven our debtors. And do not lead us into temptation, but deliver us from evil' (Matthew 6:9-13). Surely we'd expect at any one time to major on perhaps only two or three of these points as the Holy Spirit leads us.

So, 'our Father in heaven' it begins, which at once reminds us that we're on the earth and God's in heaven. What an awesome privilege that we can have, at any time, an audience with the King of Heaven! But this is an approach to God that's based on relationship. This form of address captures the intimacy of a child's relationship with its parent, and the bold asking which that can lead to, but without any undue familiarity. This is the intimate reverence of the adoring child of God, coming in a spirit of awe and worship.

Of the six points in this model prayer the first three are most definitely God-centred - dealing with God's name, God's kingdom and God's will. We could hardly be reminded more forcibly that true prayer is a concern for the glory of God. It isn't first and foremost about me getting my needs met, but about me giving God his rightful place. And when I give God his rightful place, then I'm put in my true place as I humble myself, and through prayer, express my total dependence on God in all his sovereignty over my life. This prayer acknowledges that God's on the throne - and he's holy. The first point made in the prayer is 'Hallowed be Your Name'. The Bible reminds us elsewhere that holy and revered is God's name, and we want it to be displayed that way by the way we live.

Then the words: 'Your will be done' seem to cause confusion today. Some people appear to use them at the conclusion of a specific request almost as though they were a kind of 'face-saver' just in case the desired result doesn't materialize. Others wonder why we need to bother to pray at all if God's going to do what he wants anyway. His will is sovereign after all, isn't it? What I believe these words really teach us is this: that the bottom line of all our praying has got to be: 'Do what you want in my life, LORD'. The essence of prayer is not me bending his will to mine, but it's about me bowing my will to his. Real prayer takes place when we plead in the power of the Spirit for what God desires. That requires that we be in tune with God, of course. We understand prayer best, I believe, when we understand it to be a response to his initiative. He hears and acts when our prayer is according to his will. And his Spirit moves his children into the current of God's will as they spend time in prayer.

Another thing the Lord says we should pray is: 'Give us day by day our daily bread'. The word translated 'daily' puzzled scholars for centuries. This was the only place this word occurred inside or outside the Bible. Then a few years ago, an archaeologist dug up a papyrus fragment that contained a housewife's shopping list. Next to several items the woman had scribbled this word for 'daily'. It probably meant 'enough for the coming day'. So if you pray this prayer in the morning, it's a prayer for your needs in the hours immediately ahead. Today, things are a little different in practice. In societies where fridges and freezers are commonplace we tend to do a weekly shop, but let's not forget to give thanks before each meal, recognizing that God our heavenly Father is the ultimate provider.

The relevance of this prayer request concerning daily bread can still be seen in guarding us from a spirit of independence and any selfish tendency to hoard excessively. The word 'bread' used here can refer to food in general, and we can extend the thought easily to cover all our physical and material needs. What it clearly indicates is that we're to pray for the necessities of life, and not for its luxuries. We're to ask for bread, not cake! Just the essentials to see us through the immediate future. God cares that the necessities of our material needs are met.

Next the Lord said we should pray: 'Forgive us our sins, for we also forgive everyone who is indebted to us.' Every day as we come to God in prayer, perhaps at the end of the day with the day in review, we need to come in the same spirit of repentance that the prodigal had and say 'Father, I've sinned - forgive me my sins'. When John Wesley served as a missionary to the American colonies, he had a difficult time with General James Oglethorpe. The general was known for his pride and harshness. One day Oglethorpe declared: 'I never forgive'. To which Wesley's reply was: 'then I hope you never sin'!

The Lord certainly links our experience of forgiveness with the condition that we forgive those who sin against us. Listen to his words from Mark's Gospel chapter 11 (v.25): 'Whenever you stand praying, if you have anything against anyone, forgive him, that your Father in heaven may also forgive you your trespasses.' A forgiving spirit is vital if our prayer-life is to be effective. If we refuse to forgive someone, it means we don't appreciate God's forgiveness of us. And so the Lord taught us to say: 'Forgive us our sins, for we also forgive everyone who is indebted to us'. We're never closer to God's grace than when we admit our sin and cry out for pardon. We're never more like God than when we extend forgiveness to those who have sinned against us.

If this pattern for prayer is going to be real to us, then the six great issues it contains are going to have to be things which really do matter to us in the way we live. So I have to ask myself: How important to me in everyday life is the glory of God's Name? Am I really concerned that he should rule supreme in my life? Is doing his will my heart's main desire? Do I realize my total dependence on him for everything in life? Do I mourn over my sin? And do I respond well to trial? On that last point, while it's true, that we need God's help to keep us from temptation, it does beg the question: Why would the Lord Jesus teach his followers to pray 'lead us not into temptation' when God surely would never do that anyway? Well, the word can also convey the idea of testing. When the Lord taught us to pray 'lead us not into temptation', he wasn't saying that we should ask God not to entice us with evil - for God would never do a thing like that. It seems the Lord was talking about an exemption from a kind of testing.

Sometimes testing is necessary for our own long-term good, but how much better to live so totally for the Lord, that only limited testing is called for. The request not to lead us into temptation goes on, however, to add 'but deliver us from the evil one'. Protection or immunity from harm isn't guaranteed to the Christian, but that's not to say we can't pray for it. Indeed, we must, for we find it here as part of the Lord's blueprint guiding us as to what it means in practice to pray in the will of God.

5: GETTING ACQUAINTED WITH OUR GUIDE

So, let's suppose you've recently become a Christian, and heard about the Holy Spirit. Let's begin by answering the question 'Who is the Holy Spirit?' The simple answer is that the Holy Spirit is God – that much is clear from what we can read from 1 Corinthians 2:1-16:

"And when I came to you, brethren, I did not come with superiority of speech or of wisdom, proclaiming to you the testimony of God. For I determined to know nothing among you except Jesus Christ, and Him crucified. I was with you in weakness and in fear and in much trembling, and my message and my preaching were not in persuasive words of wisdom, but in demonstration of the Spirit and of power, so that your faith would not rest on the wisdom of men, but on the power of God.

Yet we do speak wisdom among those who are mature; a

wisdom, however, not of this age nor of the rulers of this age, who are passing away; but we speak God's wisdom in a mystery, the hidden wisdom which God predestined before the ages to our glory; the wisdom which none of the rulers of this age has understood; for if they had understood it they would not have crucified the Lord of glory; but just as it is written, "Things which eye has not seen and ear has not heard, and which have not entered the heart of man, all that God has prepared for those who love him."

For to us God revealed them through the Spirit; for the Spirit searches all things, even the depths of God. For who among men knows the thoughts of a man except the spirit of the man which is in him? Even so the thoughts of God no one knows except the Spirit of God. Now we have received, not the spirit of the world, but the Spirit who is from God, so that we may know the things freely given to us by God, which things we also speak, not in words taught by human wisdom, but in those taught by the Spirit, combining spiritual thoughts with spiritual words. But a natural man does not accept the things of the Spirit of God, for they are foolishness to him; and he cannot understand them, because they are spiritually appraised. But he who is spiritual appraises all things, yet he himself is appraised by no one. For who has known the mind of the Lord, that he will instruct him? But we have the mind of Christ."

Think over what we've just read. Notice that the words 'God' and 'Spirit' are interchangeable. For example; in verses 4 & 5, the Spirit's power is also called God's power. And in verse 11 we read that the thoughts of God are fully known by the Spirit – which must make him one with God (the Father).

The second thing we need to understand is that the Holy Spirit isn't some kind of impersonal force. He reveals, searches and teaches us. "The Spirit searches all things, even the deep things of God" (v.10). Be careful with that - he doesn't have to search the depths for himself, but only so that he might reveal those same depths to us – his searching is for our sake, not his own. The Spirit knows all the thoughts of God. Didn't verse 11 say: "In the same way nobody knows the thoughts of God, except the Spirit of God" (v.11)? That's identifying the Spirit with God. His role, as described here, is to teach us what God's freely given to us.

Which leads us on nicely to what the Holy Spirit does. But, going back to the earlier verses in First Corinthians chapter 2, we also find something else he does – which is: he empowers us to share our testimony (v.1-5). In verse 3, Paul confesses that he came to the believers at Corinth in weakness, and fear and trembling. It's because we're not qualified that we're given the Spirit's power to share the gospel with others. God's done a lot for us, but the apostle Paul leaves us in no doubt as to what is the most important thing that God has done for us. "For I resolved to know nothing while I was with you except Jesus Christ and him crucified" (v.2).

And linked to that work of the cross, in Romans 5:5 and Romans 8:16, we're told that the Holy Spirit was given to us to prove God's love and his fatherhood. Just look at these verses from Romans 5: "… and hope does not disappoint, because the love of God has been poured out within our hearts through the Holy Spirit who was given to us. For while we were still helpless, at the right time Christ died for the ungodly" (Romans 5:5-6).

Notice how that takes us to the cross as the objective evidence of God's love for us. Then we read: "The Spirit Himself testifies with our spirit that we are children of God" (Romans 8:16). In this way, the Bible informs us that the Holy Spirit makes clear to us both God's redemptive work at the cross – and our relationship to God as being his children. When he was given to us, after we believed the Gospel, we were sealed (Ephesians 1:13,14) with the Holy Spirit – this thought of sealing conveys the ideas of ownership and protection as well as our final destination.

What's more, First Corinthians chapter 12, verse 13, tells us about something else which happened when we first believed in Christ as saviour. We were baptized in the Holy Spirit into a position of having eternally secure membership of Christ's (universal) Church, known as his 'body' (Matthew 16:18; Ephesians 1:22,23). The same chapter develops how the Holy Spirit has also given each of us at least one spiritual gift so as to help build up in faith or strengthen ourselves and other believers. The Bible refers to all true believers on the Lord Jesus as the 'Body of Christ.' Jesus is the head, and each of us is given a gift(s) that empowers us to function as a part of that body in some local expression of that universal church.

We know we've been born of the Spirit (John 3:3), but it's also true that he lives in us (Romans 8:9). In John 14:16-17, Jesus told his disciples that the Spirit had been **with** them and would soon be **in** them. When we're born again, the Spirit comes to reside in us so as to teach us and be our resident guide. So, let's be quite clear: all true believers have the Holy Spirit living inside them from the moment they became believers.

Jesus knows our weaknesses and that we don't have in

ourselves the strength that we need to follow him continually or to serve him, so he supplies us with the exact power we need. The Father strengthens us through the power of his Spirit in our inner being (Ephesians 3:16-17) in order to appreciate more fully Christ's love, and in the security of that knowledge, to become the mature person God wants us to become. This includes being a witness (Acts 1:8). And to be a witness, means to testify that something is true. The disciples went out testifying that Jesus was the Christ, the Son of God and Saviour of the world. When Peter and John were released from jail where they'd been held for their preaching, they gathered together with other disciples in the church and prayed. They prayed for boldness and were filled with the Holy Spirit (Acts 4:29,31).

When Paul (who was previously called Saul) was first filled with the Holy Spirit (Acts 9:17,20), he began to proclaim Jesus as the Son of God at Damascus. So it seems very clear that to be filled with the Spirit brings boldness in witnessing for Jesus. But how can we be filled with the Holy Spirit? In Luke 11:11-13, Jesus says: "Now suppose one of you fathers is asked by his son for a fish; he will not give him a snake instead of a fish, will he? "Or if he is asked for an egg, he will not give him a scorpion, will he? "If you then, being evil, know how to give good gifts to your children, how much more will your heavenly Father give the Holy Spirit to those who ask Him?"

That seems to be a simple lesson in asking and receiving, doesn't it? To attempt a very imperfect illustration, perhaps we could in some sense think reverently of the Holy Spirit as being like a power outlet in the wall of our house. The power is always there, all we have to do is plug into it – and we do that by faith. When we ask, we're to believe that God will answer our prayer.

In Ephesians 5:18, the Bible commands us to 'be filled with the Holy Spirit.' It's better translated 'be continually being filled with the Holy Spirit.' It's talking about refills or better still a habitual experience. It's not just a one-time filling, but just as we're continually in need of God's power – for example to witness, so when we ask, we get refills.

The extent to which we make choices that honour God determines how filled we are with the Holy Spirit. Being filled with the Spirit is an act of the will, a conscious desire on our part. The filling of the Holy Spirit refers to our yielding our lives to be under God's gracious control. So, in a sense the filling of the Spirit is not so much us having more of him, but it's about us allowing him to have more of us – more of our life submitted to his control. This seems contradictory and is at odds with the prevailing world-view: giving up control of your life in order to be in control … but it's a clear Biblical concept … even as Jesus himself expressed it in Matthew 10:39 – "Whoever finds his life will lose it, and whoever loses his life for my sake will find it." (NIV)

Finally, a major concern of the Holy Spirit is to transform us to be like Christ. "But we all, with unveiled face, beholding as in a mirror the glory of the Lord, are being transformed into the same image from glory to glory, just as from the Lord, the Spirit" (2 Corinthians 3:18). He also helps us to overcome the power of sin and evil, and he promotes unity among believers on the Lord, but these are topics for following chapters.

6: ENJOYING CHRISTIAN FELLOWSHIP

Earlier in this book, we touched on the fact that at the moment we receive Christ as saviour by personal faith, we're immersed in the Spirit into Christ's universal church, which is biblically referred to being as 'his body.' From then on it's important that each new believer is encouraged to get the best out of 'Body life' within the supportive context of the local church.

In practice, this'll mean following positive role models within that local church setting. The Bible hints at just such an informal mentoring policy when it mentions on occasions those who are 'examples' or "ensamples" to others. Some of the believers in the early local church of God in Thessalonica were spoken about in that way, so let's first pick up some points from there which will serve as a little revision, starting with the example of praying.

We read in vv. 1 Thessalonians 1:1,2 that "we give thanks mentioning you in our prayers constantly ..." God wants our prayers to be so much more than prayers for food and health, as we can see if we read through any of Paul's Bible prayers. Early African converts to Christianity were serious about praying. Each had a separate spot in the woods where he would pray. The paths to these became well worn. If someone began to neglect prayer, it was soon apparent to the others who said: "Brother, the grass grows on your path." It's good when a more established Christian can model for us how to be intentional and deliberate in prayer (Paul prayed 'bearing in mind ...' in our earlier verse), making it a planned act of getting away from stuff, noise and agendas.

In Mark 1:36-39 we read about how the disciples disturbed Jesus' own early morning prayer time one day with the words: "Everyone is looking for you!" As if that was more important than prayer! After all, it's the Father who sets the mission agenda, not us. In fact, prayer saves time because it clarifies what's important and what's urgent, and spares us a lot of things that're unnecessary. To find your sense of direction and the courage to do what's essential – be sure not to let the grass grow on your (prayer) path!

The believers at Thessalonica were also Bible-oriented, and in vv. 1:5,6 we read (that they received) "the gospel in word and power and the Spirit and full conviction". In other words, God's Word was being received with joy for what it really is: the Word of God. Someone – James M. Gray – has shared: "On one occasion, when I was on a short vacation, I took a pocket edition of Ephesians with me. Lying down one afternoon, I read all six chapters. My interest was so aroused that I read the entire epistle again. In fact, I did not finally lay it down until I had gone through it some 15 times." He then said, "When I arose to go into the house, I was in possession of Ephesians; or better yet, it was in possession of me. I had the feeling that I had been lifted up to sit together in heavenly places with Christ Jesus - a feeling that was new to me." This testimony encouraged Gray to saturate his mind and heart with God's Word so that he could freely communicate it to others. We should read the Bible to pursue God; to live in integrity; to develop respect for the Bible; and to help overcome opposition.

Back at Thessalonica, Paul and his preaching companions spoke (in 1 Thessalonians 1:5) of "the kind of men we proved to be among you". This brings us to modelling authentic lives to each other. Someone has written on the topic of getting along with people, that the SIX most important words are: "I admit I made a mistake." The FIVE most important words: "You did a good job." The FOUR most important words: "What do you think?" The THREE most important words: "After you, please." The TWO most important words: "Thank you." The ONE most important word: "We" (with the LEAST important word being: "I").

First Thessalonians chapter 2 expands on this good advice by saying that Paul and his companions were gentle, affectionate, hard-working, devout, upright, blameless, encouragers, sometimes like a father, sometimes like a mother – that's what we should each contribute to a genuine Christian fellowship which incubates new life. And new Christians should commit to avail themselves of such warm Christian fellowship at every opportunity they can. The very first local Christian fellowship, the Church of God at Jerusalem, about which we read in Acts 2, certainly did that.

When we look at v.41, we see that the step after believer's

baptism is the step of addition to the fellowship of God's people locally. Far from this being something we take upon ourselves, these Bible passages make it clear this is the Lord's initiative in our hearts – one which, at a human level, we have a duty to respond to. And once added to that church fellowship, the first Christians found themselves in a fellowship which really functioned; as well as being involved in learning that lived; praying that powered; and worship that warmed. When persecution came, they supported each other in prayer (Acts 12:5). When problems came that threatened their unity, they looked to one another by God's help for the solutions (Acts 6:1-6; 15:1-31). They were clearly inter-dependent. They needed each other, just as we need each other.

The story is told of the effect upon others of the absence of a believer from church gatherings. The man concerned had faithfully been in attendance every week for many years, but for the past couple of weeks had been absent. One of the other believers decided to pay the man a visit at his small cottage. Upon knocking, the door was opened almost immediately – as if the occupant had been expecting a visit. After exchanging pleasantries they both sat down beside the open fire in the living room, which brought a welcome warmth to the situation. Nothing was said. They both just sat there, gazing into the vivid amber glow of the fire. This took away any awkwardness. After a few minutes, the visitor reached forward and with some tongs carefully removed a glowing, red-hot ember and placed it on the hearth stone beside the fire.

Both men fixed their gaze on it, watching as its glow faded so that all that was left was a charred, black coal. He then took the tongs again and placed the coal back into the fire, where it immediately began to glow again, until it again became red-hot. Another minute or two passed, then the visiting brother got up and made his way to the door. The house-owner helped him on with his coat. Not a word had been said since they sat down in front of the fire but, with tears in his eyes, the man simply looked at him and said, "Thank you so much for visiting and thank you for your fiery sermon. I'll see you back at church again next Sunday."

As we said, you and I need each other. When we try to 'go it alone', or when we don't give priority to being with fellow-believers, the glow of our love, enthusiasm and commitment to the Lord rapidly fades and grows cold. How often have you been encouraged by a fellow-disciple's joy in the Lord? How often have you received the sound, wise advice of an older Christian? How many times have you been helped and comforted through some difficult situation by the shared experience of another Christian? It was surely like that in the first Christian communities – which were described biblically as those who 'belonged to the Way' – the original and prescribed way of Christian discipleship.

After all, we were created by God to be inter-dependent, not independent. All God's revealed purposes in the past through Abraham to Moses and beyond were centred on the establishment of a community of believers who would come together in unity of heart and purpose - in close relationship not only with each other, but also with God – so close in fact that God repeatedly referred to them as 'My people' in the Old Testament.

It's not the least bit surprising, then, to find that same value and importance given to the idea of 'community' in the New Testament, among those who believed in the Lord Jesus Christ. We're first introduced to it, as we say, in Acts chapter 2 where we also read: "Those who had received his word were baptized; and that day there were added about three thousand souls. They were continually devoting themselves to the apostles' teaching and to [the] fellowship, to the breaking of bread and to [the] prayer[s]."

This was the beginning of something that would develop right through the New Testament writings. Everywhere on the pages of the New Testament we meet those who belong to a well-defined community of born-again disciples, all baptized by immersion in water, all added locally to church of God fellowship, all serving according to one pattern of teaching in every place, all maintained under a fellowship of elders while being separated to God. If we're to follow their example, then there'll be no room for a 'lowest common denominator' approach even today. Was it not our Lord's expressed desire for his followers "that they may all be one" (John 17:20-23)? Unity like this can only be reached through a sincere commitment on our part to carefully follow the pattern the Lord laid down in His Word (see Romans 6:17; 2 Timothy 1:13).

God calls us as individuals, it's true, but then he shows us in the Bible how we should come together with other believers who have the same desire to follow the Lord obediently (Acts 2:41,42). The unity we've been emphasizing is really important to the Lord – so important, in fact, he even spoke about it as he was going out to die. Now, if that's the case, shouldn't we make sure we're in a community today that corresponds exactly with that first Christian community of those who 'belonged to the Way'?

Before we conclude this section on enjoying Christian fellowship, let's return to the church fellowship at Thessalonica, where we noted that the term 'examples' was used. We've so far traced how prayer and Quiet Times, valuing and reading the Bible, and leading authentic lives of supportive fellowship were being modelled at Thessalonica. Let's conclude this chapter by reminding ourselves how they were also exemplary in their witnessing.

Verse 1:8 says, "the word of the Lord has sounded out from you". Martin Buber, the Jewish philosopher, recalls: "My grandfather was lame. Once they asked him to tell a story about his teacher, and he related how his master used to hop and dance while he prayed. My grandfather rose as he spoke and was so swept away by his story that he himself began to hop and dance to show how the master had done. From that hour he was cured of his lameness." When we tell the story of our Master, we too experience his power. Do tell your story to others again and again!

7: HOW TO LIVE VICTORIOUSLY AS A CHRISTIAN

No guidance for new Christians would ever be complete without some guidance about how to defeat evil, and so how to live victoriously as a Christian. The last chapter of the Apostle Paul's letter to the Ephesians is about how to equip ourselves in order to live defensively. As a new Christian, we need to be aware that the Devil is real, and realize we're going to feel a new sense of opposition in our lives, along with the strain of sustaining 'right' behaviour. A lot of new Christians struggle with this – as they naively thought – or were led to think – that life would be altogether wonderful once they had received Christ. But the Bible realistically informs us that Christians will experience opposition. Thankfully, it also tells us how to withstand and resist in God-given power, and gives us an awareness of what lies behind temptation and trials (James 1). Beyond the early burst of enthusiasm, we need a biblical dose of realism in order to stay the course in long-term commitment.

It's in chapter 4 that we begin to get the really practical teaching of Paul's letter to the Ephesians. The doctrinal outline which precedes it simply has to make a difference in how we live our lives. And, I also want you to notice that the practical teaching of chapters 4 and 5 comes before the discussion of spiritual warfare in chapter 6. The actual battleground is set out in chapters 4 and 5, and it relates to our behaviours and relationships.

With that scene-setting, let's have a look now at Ephesians, chapter 6, where we read from verse 10: "Finally, be strong in the Lord and in the strength of His might. Put on the full armor of God, so that you will be able to stand firm against the schemes of the devil. For our struggle is not against flesh and blood, but against the rulers, against the powers, against the world forces of this darkness, against the spiritual forces of wickedness in the heavenly places.

Therefore, take up the full armor of God, so that you will be able to resist in the evil day, and having done everything, to stand firm. Stand firm therefore, having girded your loins with truth, and having put on the breastplate of righteousness, and having shod your feet with the preparation of the gospel of peace; in addition to all, taking up the shield of faith with which you will be able to extinguish all the flaming arrows of the evil *one.* and take the helmet of salvation, and the sword of the Spirit, which is the word of God. With all prayer and petition pray at all times in the Spirit, and with this in view, be on the alert." (Ephesians 6:10-18)

What's going on here in the Bible text? The context is set as our having to be strong by God's help for the spiritual battle which rages against the forces of evil. We're used to virtual reality – the war games we play with our thumbs – but this is for real! The value of our Christian life for God depends on us understanding this information! So, let's have a closer look.

At verse 14, the command to 'stand firm therefore' should be seen as an urgent command. In verses 14, 15 & 16 there are 4 words which go on to describe what's meant – i.e. how we're to stand. These words are: having girded; having put on; having shod; taking up. You'll see they each relate to 1 of 4 pieces of armour. Then v.17 starts a new point with a fresh command. I'd like us to concentrate on the first of those descriptions just mentioned; and the first way in which we're called upon to stand – which is by buckling on our belt. To begin with, we need to think of the background to the Apostle Paul's writing at this point. He was in prison, guarded by Roman soldiers, and he was using what was right there before him as an analogy for the spiritual battle he wanted us to be clued into.

So, we need to think about a Roman soldier and his belt. Before a Roman soldier put on his armour, he put a belt around his waist. To be able to examine the belt properly we have to get rid of our 20th century ideas about belts and we need to try to put ourselves back into the first century. Back then, when you got dressed you would put on your 'loin cloth' – which was like an oversized diaper (called a "nappy" in the UK!). Then you would put on your undergarment, which was basically a long baggy shirt. After that you would put on your cloak. Basically this process meant you had all this baggy clothing hanging off you - which is why you needed your belt. It would be used to gather all that loose clothing together and hold it in place so that it wouldn't get in the way when you were walking around. The belt also served to hold the bottom of the breastplate in place - and to hold the sheath for the sword. If the belt wasn't in place you'd always be in danger of tripping over your own clothing and certainly not ready for battle. Everything depended on the belt being right – or the rest was useless.

Okay, good. So much for the background information we need to make sense of this. But let's try now to get to grips with the actual teaching. The Apostle Paul repeatedly talks about 'standing firm.' We've absolutely got to take a stand as a Christian, and there's something - pictured or represented as a belt - the first thing we need to get right ... but what is that in our case? Well, the belt is called the belt of truth so that's a clue, a massive clue, but 'truth' can be a description of actual facts or it can refer to a state of genuineness or there again, 'truth' also plays a major part in integrity. So when we buckle on the belt of truth what are we doing? Are we buckling up a set of facts? Are we talking about whether or not we're genuine Christians? Or, is it an issue of being people of integrity?

Everything in the context informs us that truth here refers to a believer's integrity (which means his or her dependability and faithfulness). As a soldier's belt or sash gave ease and freedom of movement, so our personal integrity gives us freedom – freedom with self, others, and God – and that's vital for every Christian.

We all know what's meant by 'integrity', but perhaps a concrete example wouldn't harm. One of the best golfers in history, Bobby Jones, was in the rough, at the 1925 U.S. Open when he reported that his ball moved as he addressed it. Without that one-shot penalty, he would have won outright. Instead, Jones finished in a tie with Willie Macfarlane, and lost in a playoff. He scoffed at praise for his sportsmanship. "You might as well praise me for not breaking into banks," Jones said. "There is only one way to play this game." And there's only one way to live victoriously as a Christian. Integrity means doing the right thing, even when nobody is watching. Integrity means doing the right thing, even when others around us are not doing right things. Integrity means doing the right thing when others misunderstand and criticise us. It's something that's broader than honesty – honesty is about facts; but integrity is about principles. And, as Christians, we're to be all about living by Bible principles.

Next was the Breastplate of Righteousness which was light in weight and gave ease of movement as well as protection from blows. It was anchored to the belt, from above. In Proverbs 4:23, we're taught to guard our heart with all diligence for out of it flows our whole life. The decisions we make determine the outcome of our life. How vital then that we choose to do what is right, not what is popular, and not what we can get away with.

Then our feet are to be fitted with readiness. Some historians credit their footwear as one of the reasons why the Roman Army was so dominant. It was equipped with spikes on the soles to provide soldiers with grip, strong stance and a good balance – all of which gave them a superior posture in battles typically fought on uneven terrain. We need to have a good grip of, and take a firm stand on, Gospel truth. Satan will try to back us into situations to wrong-foot us. Let's not slip up on the fundamentals of the Gospel and of the Christian Faith.

And so we come to the shield of faith. The Romans had a long, rectangular, knees-to-chin shield which protected them from spears, and it could be knelt behind if arrows were raining in on them. Groups of soldiers who were besieging a town could close ranks in formation and hold their shields over their heads to make a huge cover to protect the whole group from fiery arrows. The Roman shield pictures the faith of the believer in the promises of God, while reminding us of the benefits of keeping in step with others around us.

Next there's the helmet of salvation. The Romans had the best helmet of the ancient world. Originally made of animal skin, it was strengthened with bronze or other metal, and topped with a horsehair crest, with a visor to protect the face. The greatest battle is in our minds. This is the area that the enemy most wants to attack. He wants to damage our assured hope of salvation – to cause us to doubt. The Bible encourages us to prepare our minds for action (1 Peter 1:13), and set them on things above (Colossians 3:2).

Finally, the sword of the Spirit – probably referring to the two-edged sword. Its advantage was that the soldier didn't have to turn his sword round to inflict damage to the enemy. Our sword of the Spirit is the Word of God. When Jesus was tempted by Satan in the wilderness, he quoted scripture. Overall then, may God help us to stand firm on the promises of his Word, and – remembering the battleground charted out by Ephesians chapters 4 & 5 – let's be sure to live defensively and victoriously by maintaining purity and submissiveness in our relationships!

8: HOW TO STAY ACTIVELY INVOLVED

The first people ever to become Christians didn't just sit around on their hands. Even skim-reading the New Testament ought to convince us that life in a first century Church of God was no arm-chair spectator sport where everyone sat around and watched a few professional Christian leaders do all the work of mission and ministry.

In three places mainly, the Apostle Paul describes how God has equipped every true Christian believer to play an active role. These three places are Romans chapter 12; First Corinthians chapter 12; and Ephesians chapter 4. These list various gifts or functions, most of which are still applicable today. Paul tells us (Ephesians 4:11,12) that these are provided so that we can be equipped in serving the Lord in a hands-on way.

Practically nothing will improve your service and enhance your fulfilment as dramatically as discovering, developing and discharging your own spiritual gift. This is the way to maximising your effectiveness; while at the same time minimising your stress, which is obviously good. Our mentor, or other mature Christian whom we know well, should be able to guide and confirm to us the indications we ourselves may have already picked up as to what our gift(s) may be. And those indications will likely include such things as the feedback we have received; wherever we have found an appropriate sense of joyful satisfaction in service; any focus which has habitually developed in our praying; and the way our thoughts tend to be led as we read our Bible.

Now, often one of the first areas of service is sharing what's happened to us with our friends and colleagues. It's not uncommon to feel somewhat embarrassed in doing this, as we anticipate awkwardness or a dismissive reaction on their part. It's not that we are ashamed of our testimony, but we are very conscious of messing up as we try to explain what has happened to us. How can we overcome embarrassment, and so electrify the fence on which our friends sit? Well, it's good to practice ahead of time how we can share our story effectively with others. Sometimes we need a bit of a nudge to get us out of our 'Circle of Comfort' and into the 'Zone of the Unknown'. Have we experienced 'Spirit-directed promptings' to do just that? (cf. Acts 8:26; 16:6-9). If not, might it be because we don't begin each day with a prayer like: 'Use me to point someone to You today – I promise to cooperate in any way I can. If You want me to say a word for You today, I'll try to do that'?

Then we need to be ready with a simple '3D' strategy: first the need to **d**evelop friendships; then over time – but not too much time – we try to **d**iscover their stories; and then – a third 'd' – we pray about **d**iscerning the next steps – that could be an invitation or offering a book or CD or even just sharing our story. That means we need to have our own '3-pronged story' ready.

I call it 3-pronged because it should be in 3 parts: what our life was like before we encountered Jesus; how that encounter happened; and what life is like for us now. To prepare your story, try answering what we might well anticipate our friend's question will be: 'Why is all this God stuff important to you?' Try to prepare an answer to that question without long-windedness, without fuzziness, without incomprehensible jargon, or any sense of superiority in 45 seconds - or in less than 100 words. Don't worry if that takes you longer than you think! Beyond that, it's good to research some answers to the usual questions which always come up, like 'what about those who've never heard of Christ?'; 'how could a God of love send anyone to 'hell'?'; 'isn't it all psychological anyway?' etc. You'll find there are only about 8 of these typical questions. Alongside the answers, have a small stock of tried and tested illustrations, ready to use.

Once having introduced someone to the Christian faith, this will inevitably raise for them the same question it had already raised for you: is there a particular way to serve and worship God today – one which is endorsed by the Lord in the Bible? Well, what did Paul say? Paul said 'according to the Way which they call a sect, I ... serve ... God' (24:14). These words are found in Acts 24 verse 14 and quite obviously they're talking about the original biblical way of Christian service and worship. If we look in either the Old or New Testament of our Bible, we find that the public service or public worship of God is closely linked with the subject of God's house on earth. For example, the letter to the Hebrews has a lot to teach us about such worship, and it links us back to the time of Moses when it says in Hebrews 3:5-6:

"Moses was faithful in all His house as a servant, for a testimony of those things which were to be spoken later; but Christ [is faithful] as a Son over [God's] house, whose house we are, if we hold fast our confidence and the boast of our hope firm until the end."

The best place to start would seem to be by clarifying what exactly is meant by 'God's house?' Nowadays this expression means different things to different people – for example, any place for public worship (usually Christian) may be referred to as a house of God - so it's important to be clear on the actual Bible meaning. The writer of this Bible letter tells the people for whom this letter was originally intended that they're God's house – in fact, linking himself with the readership, he says 'whose house we are'. So it's no longer a physical house or building: 'whose house we are,' he says - and then he adds the condition: 'if we hold fast ...'

This condition is something he says a lot more about, later in this letter. There's talk of the danger of 'falling away', for example, in Hebrews chapter 6, verse 6. Now, let me say this very carefully: if God's house comprises everyone who's known salvation through faith in Christ, then this 'falling away' means falling away from salvation. For if to have a place in God's house means receiving Christ's salvation – and only that - then falling away from God's house can only mean losing that same salvation.

But the Bible does NOT teach that, once saved, we can be lost again. Therefore, God's house has simply got to be distinguished from the vast company of all those who've ever known salvation by God's grace through personal faith in Jesus Christ, and is also to be distinguished even from all currently living believers. The Bible deals with the security of our salvation in so many ways as to put beyond the shadow of a doubt the fact that we can never, never be lost again, after having believed in Christ for salvation, the salvation which is from the penalty which our sins deserve.

Which shows us that the defining issue for a place in God's house is not the possession of salvation, for although Hebrews tells us we can fall away from God's house, yet we can never be dispossessed of our salvation. There's no need whatsoever for us to hold fast to our salvation, for the Lord Jesus himself holds us fast, and assures us that no one can snatch us away from him. But, regarding what's called God's house, we evidently do need to hold fast, just as they did, to whom the author of Hebrews wrote some two thousand years ago.

All those who have ever at some point come to saving faith in Christ include myriads of believers who are now dead. But God's house at any time does not even include all true living believers, for there's that condition applied: 'if we hold fast ...' The Hebrews' letter was written as its name implies, to early Jewish Christians – the very first Christians being, of course, Jews. They had left behind the ceremonial Law of Moses to embrace Jesus as the Messiah, and so follow the teaching of his apostles. And following the apostles' teaching brought them into the New Testament Churches of God. The Book of the Acts of the Apostles tells us how this came about. These churches spread outwards from Jerusalem mainly as a result of the various missionary journeys of the Apostle Paul. There isn't the slightest evidence that some practised baptism while others didn't; no indication whatsoever that some churches had elders whereas others had a different form of government. They all served God according to the (one) Way (which was then regarded as a sect by mainstream Judaism, see Acts 24:14).

They were a persecuted community then. It's clear from Paul's words earlier, that there was a stigma associated with belonging to 'the Way.' And some of them - by the time that the letter to the Hebrews came to be written - some of them had come to feel life would be easier outside of 'the (Christian) Way.' They felt life would be simpler again if, as in the old days, they were just going along with the Law of Moses like the majority of folks around them, at least in Israel.

To people just like that, to those who were wavering on the brink of leaving the community of first century churches of God, the writer of the Hebrews' letter makes his appeal by the Spirit of God: 'don't go back; don't fall away.' To quit their association with 'the Way' would not mean the loss of their salvation, but – and this is the main point of the entire letter – they would miss out on everything that was special in serving God together in the biblical community of Churches of God. It would be a falling away in terms of their service – and from the privileges and responsibilities which attended it. In short, they would lose their place in God's house – they wouldn't lose their salvation, remember – but they'd lose their place in God's house.

That clearly defined visible community of believers, as described in the pages of the New Testament, was where God lived by his Spirit, in a way that answered exactly to earlier eras when the place where God lived on earth – his house – was known as Moses' Tabernacle or Solomon's Temple. That was always *the one* place at any one time for the corporate worship of God's people. In the Old Testament it had a physical expression, but now 'we worship in spirit and truth' (John 4:23,24) which surely minimises physical aspects while appreciating the wonderful spiritual experience this is (take time, please, to check out Hebrews 12:22 ff. & Hebrews 9:24; Hebrews 10:19).

Finally, before I leave this topic on becoming active and staying active in serving the Lord, it's important we should be equipped to spot false teachings and other unhelpful ideas, for sooner rather than later, we're likely to run up against them as we start actively sharing our faith with others. If you come across someone who seems to be saying something rather different, try asking them: what's your ultimate authority?; who do you say Jesus is?; how are you telling people to get right with God?

By now, you know the clear, obvious answers to these questions. If there's any hesitation or equivocation about the answers they give, you'll know straight away that something is far from right. May the Lord help you to stay active and strong for him – avoiding what's wrong and enthusiastically following what's right!

FURTHER TITLES IN THIS SERIES

I f you've enjoyed reading this book, first of all please consider taking a moment to leave a positive review on Amazon! Secondly, you may be interested to know that, at the date of the publishing of this book, the Search For Truth library now stands at almost 50 titles; each contains excellent reading material in a down-to-earth and conversational style, covering a wide range of topics from Bible character studies, theme studies, book studies, apologetics, prophecy, Christian living and more. The simplest way to access this material for purchase is by visiting Brian's Amazon author page:

- Amazon.com: http://amzn.to/1u7rzIA
- Amazon.co.uk: http://amzn.to/YZt5zC

Alternatively, the books can also be found simply by searching for the specific title or "Search For Truth Series" on Amazon. Paperback versions can also be purchased from Hayes Press at www.hayespress.org.

A flavour of some of the books in the library are below:

Healthy Churches: God's Bible Blueprint For Growth
As Brian notes in the opening chapters of this book, many churches in the Western world seem to be declining in numbers and spiritual vitality. He explores some of the root causes and also how this trend could be reversed. The good news, as Brian reminds us, is that God gives us the growth blueprint in His Word through a number of key Bible words, such as sowing, reaping, planting, watering, cultivating, building and edifying. Find out the importance of each step in the process and get inspired to go for growth with, in and through, God!

Overcoming Objections to Christian Faith
This book provides a concise introduction to answering 10 key objections to the Christian faith by giving a number of insightful illustrations and Biblical references which all Christians can use to help them give "a reason for the hope that is within us" and whet the appetite for further research on each question in greater depth:

- Why do the innocent suffer?
- Don't all religions lead to God?
- What about the heathen?
- Isn't the Christian experience only psychological?
- Are the miracles possible?
- Isn't the Bible full of errors?
- Won't a good life get me to heaven?
- How can you believe in hell and a God of love?
- Hasn't science done away with the need for faith?
- What about all the bloodshed in the name of religion?

Praying With Paul

Prayer is one of the greatest assets that a Christian could possess, but sometimes it seems to be a real challenge to make it a full part of our devotional life. Brian examines the way the great prayer warrior himself - the apostle Paul - approached prayer. What were the key things that Paul prayed about and how did he do it? Paul was an expert in how to have a productive prayer life with real intimacy with God. There's no better example of the practice of prayer that we can follow - may it challenge us all to a more productive prayer life in the secret place! A bonus book, Passing the Baton, also features in this book, and takes a look at 4 important relationships in the Bible and the handover of service for God from one to the other.

Unlocking Hebrews

The letter to the Hebrews has been called "the forgotten letter of the New Testament". But, as Brian outlines in this little book, the letter contains a marvellous, divine revelation that is not found anywhere else in the Bible! The writer of the letter is concerned that new believers might be soon be walking away from their new-found faith and reverting back to Judaism. He passionately explains through a series of "warnings" exactly what they will be missing, the unique superiority of Jesus Christ, but also an amazing insight into the location of the collective worship of God, which remains unchanged 2,000 years later!

James – The Epistle of Straw?

Martin Luther didn't seem overly impressed with the Bible letter by James, describing it as 'a right strawy epistle'! It seems he felt disappointed that it didn't contain any exalted description of Christ, nor make reference to the work of the Spirit, and didn't work hard to defend the faith. It's true that James doesn't deal with the glories of Christ and his Church or with the great Christian blessings, nor does he transport us to the world to come. James seems to be at home in more mundane matters. He doesn't write in great soaring passages, nor are there many strongly motivating exhortations. But the value of his contribution, under God, is in forcing us to face up squarely to practical realities and their ethical implications. Brian Johnston, brings us face to face with these realities in a down to earth style that perhaps James himself would have appreciated!

Other Titles

- Answers to Listeners Questions
- An Unchanging God?
- The Kingdom of God – Past, Present or Future?
- Edge of Eternity – Approaching The End Of Life
- God's Appointment Calendar: The Feasts of Jehovah
- Seeds – A Potted Bible History
- AWOL! Bible Deserters and Defectors
- 5 Sacred Solos – The Truths That The Reformation Recovered
- Salt & The Sacrifice of Christ
- Turning The World Upside Down – Seven Revolutionary Ideas That Changed The World
- Windows To Faith
- The Visions of Zechariah
- The Last Words of Jesus
- Closer Than A Brother – Christian Friendship
- Experiencing God in Ephesians
- About The Bush – The Five Excuses of Moses
- Trees of the Bible
- Once Saved, Always Saved?
- After God's Own Heart: The Life of David
- Knowing God: Reflections on Psalm 23
- Jesus: What Does The Bible Really Say?

- No Compromise!
- Abraham: Friend Of God
- Jesus: Son Over God's House
- The Way: New Testament Discipleship
- The Tabernacle: God's House of Shadows
- Esther: A Date With Destiny
- Power Outage: Christianity Unplugged
- Five Woman And A Baby: The Genealogy of Jesus
- Bible Answers For Big Questions
- Samson: A Type Of Christ
- Fencepost Turtles: People Placed By God
- Hope For Humanity – God's Fix For A Broken World
- Tribes & Tribulations – Israel's Predicted Personalities
- Legacy Of Kings – Israel's Chequered History
- Life, the Universe and Ultimate Answers
- The Supremacy of Christ – A Bible Study of Jesus
- The Glory of God
- An Unchanging God: Exploring The Allegation Of Divine Inconsistency
- Pure Christianity: The Essence of Biblical Discipleship
- Living in God's House: His Design in Action
- Double Vision: The Insights of Isaiah
- They Met At The Cross: Five Encounters With Jesus
- Tomorrow's Headlines: Unlocking Bible Prophecy

SEARCH FOR TRUTH RADIO BROADCASTS

Search for Truth Radio has been a ministry of the Churches of God (see www.churchesofgod.info) since 1978. Free Search for Truth podcasts can be listened to online or downloaded at four locations:

- At SFT's own dedicated podcast site: www.searchfortruth.podbean.com
- Via Itunes using the podcast app (search for Search For Truth)
- On the Churches of God website: (**http://www.churchesofgod.info**)
- On the Transworld Radio website: (http://www.twr360.org/programs/ministry_id,103)

If you have enjoyed reading one of our books or listening to a radio broadcast, we would love to know about that, or answer any questions that you might have. Contact us at:

- The Barn, Flaxlands, Royal Wootton Bassett, Wiltshire, UK SN4 8DY
- P.O. Box 748, Ringwood, Victoria 3134, Australia
- P.O. Box 70115, Chilomoni, Blantyre, Malawi
- Web site: www.searchfortruth.org.uk
- Email: sft@churchesofgod.info

ABOUT THE AUTHOR

Responding to God's call in his life Brian Johnston left his post as a UK government scientist in 1987 to become a fulltime Bible teacher and evangelist on behalf of the Churches of God (**www.churchesofgod.info**). For many years, he has been spending much of his time in missionary church-planting activity in Belgium and the Philippines. He also anchors Search for Truth Radio and is an editor of Needed Truth magazine (see **www.neededtruth.info**). He has authored the book Exploring Issues of Life. He is married to Rosemary, and they have two children, Michael and Anna.